The Middle Child Syndrome

Copyright Page

TITLE: The Middle Child Syndrome

1ST Edition

Table of Contents

The Middle Child Syndrome

By Roberto Miguel Rodriguez

Chapter 1: The Middle Child Syndrome: Understanding the Psychological Effects

The Concept of Middle Child Syndrome

In the realm of birth order psychology, the concept of Middle Child Syndrome has garnered significant attention over the years. As educators, it is crucial for us to understand the psychological effects associated with this phenomenon in order to better support and nurture the middle-born individuals in our care.

Middle Child Syndrome refers to the sense of neglect, insignificance, or perceived disadvantage experienced by middle children within their families. While birth order may seem like a trivial factor, numerous studies have shown that it can have a profound impact on an individual's development, personality, and overall well-being.

Understanding the unique traits exhibited by middle children is a key aspect of our role as educators. Middle-born individuals often develop a set of characteristics that distinguish them from their siblings and shape their identity. By examining these traits, such as adaptability, diplomacy, and independence, we can tailor our teaching strategies to meet their specific needs.

Sibling rivalry is a common occurrence in middle childhood, and it can have lasting psychological implications. As educators, we must be equipped with effective resolution strategies to help middle children navigate and overcome this rivalry, fostering healthy relationships with their siblings.

The formation of middle child identity is another crucial aspect to consider. By exploring the role of birth order on self-perception, we can gain insights into how middle children view themselves and how they fit into their family dynamic. This understanding can guide us in promoting a positive self-image and a sense of belonging for middle-born students.

Moreover, parenting strategies play a significant role in nurturing the psychological well-being of middle children. Educators can collaborate with parents to develop effective techniques that foster a supportive and empowering environment for middle-born individuals.

In the context of peer relationships, middle children often face unique social dynamics and challenges. Understanding these dynamics can enable us to provide appropriate guidance and support to help middle-born students navigate social situations and develop healthy friendships.

Success and achievement are important aspects of every child's life. Investigating the factors that contribute to achievement in middle-born individuals can help us identify strategies to promote their academic and personal growth.

Communication is a fundamental skill, and birth order can influence how middle children express themselves verbally and non-verbally. Analyzing this impact can guide us in creating an inclusive and supportive communication environment for middle-born students.

Middle children often face adversity, and their ability to cope and develop resilience is crucial. By studying how middle children cope with challenges, we can implement effective strategies to support their resilience-building process.

Finally, examining the empathetic abilities and characteristics of middle-born individuals can shed light on their unique strengths and contributions. By fostering empathy in the classroom, we can cultivate a compassionate and inclusive learning environment for all students.

In conclusion, understanding the concept of Middle Child Syndrome is vital for educators. By delving into the psychological effects associated with birth order, we can develop strategies to support the unique needs of middle-born students. From addressing sibling rivalry to promoting resilience and empathy, our role as educators extends beyond academics to nurturing the psychological well-being of every child in our care.

Historical Overview of Middle Child Syndrome Studies

The study of the middle child syndrome has a long and fascinating history, with researchers and psychologists delving into the psychological effects of being a middle child for many decades. This subchapter aims to provide educators with a comprehensive understanding of the historical development of middle child syndrome studies, shedding light on the insights gained over the years.

Early studies on birth order, conducted in the early 20th century, laid the foundation for understanding the unique traits associated with middle-born individuals. These studies initially focused on the general characteristics of birth order, but it was not until the mid-20th century that researchers started to specifically examine the middle child's experiences.

During the 1960s and 1970s, psychologists began to explore the concept of sibling rivalry and its implications for middle children. These studies highlighted the psychological challenges faced by middle children due to their position in the birth order hierarchy. They also identified specific resolution strategies that educators and parents could employ to mitigate these challenges and foster positive sibling relationships.

In the 1980s and 1990s, researchers turned their attention to middle child identity formation. They sought to understand how birth order influenced self-perception and the development of a middle child's sense of identity. These studies shed light on the unique struggles and strengths of middle-born individuals in shaping their self-concept.

As the field progressed, researchers started investigating the impact of birth order on various aspects of a middle child's life. Studies explored the strategies for nurturing the psychological well-being of middle children, the social dynamics and challenges they face in peer relationships, and the factors that contribute to their achievement and success.

More recent research has focused on communication patterns among middle-born individuals, analyzing the impact of birth order on both verbal and non-verbal expression. These studies have revealed interesting insights into how birth order influences communication styles and preferences.

Additionally, researchers have explored middle children's resilience, studying how they cope with adversity and develop resilience. They have also examined the empathetic abilities and characteristics of middle-born individuals, uncovering unique empathetic traits specific to this birth order.

In conclusion, the historical overview of middle child syndrome studies demonstrates the evolution of research in this field, highlighting the increasing focus on understanding the psychological effects of being a middle child. Educators play a crucial role in supporting middle-born students, and this chapter aims to equip them with the knowledge and insights necessary to better understand the experiences and needs of middle children in the educational setting.

The Impact of Birth Order on Middle Child Syndrome

Introduction:

In this subchapter, we will explore the psychological effects of birth order on middle children, specifically focusing on the phenomenon known as Middle Child Syndrome. As educators, it is crucial for us to understand how birth order shapes our students' experiences and influences their psychological well-being. By delving into this topic, we can better support middle children in our classrooms and create an inclusive and nurturing environment for them.

Understanding Middle Child Syndrome:

Middle Child Syndrome refers to the unique set of psychological challenges that middle-born individuals face due to their birth order. They often feel overlooked, overshadowed, and neglected in comparison to their older and younger siblings. This can lead to feelings of insecurity, low self-esteem, and a desire to seek attention in unconventional ways.

Factors Contributing to Middle Child Syndrome:

Several factors contribute to the development of Middle Child Syndrome. First, middle children often struggle to find their identity within the family dynamic, as they are neither the responsible oldest nor the pampered youngest. This struggle with identity formation can lead to feelings of confusion and frustration. Additionally, middle children frequently experience heightened sibling rivalry, as they compete for attention and validation from their parents.

Effects on Psychological Well-being:

The impact of Middle Child Syndrome on middle children's psychological well-being is significant. They may develop a sense of inadequacy and perceive themselves as less capable or successful than their siblings. These feelings can manifest in academic performance, social relationships, and overall self-perception. Educators play a crucial role in recognizing and addressing these issues to support middle children in reaching their full potential.

Strategies for Educators:

As educators, we can implement various strategies to nurture the psychological well-being of middle children. These include creating an inclusive classroom environment, providing opportunities for middle children to express themselves and showcase their talents, and encouraging positive sibling relationships. By acknowledging their unique traits and strengths, we can help middle children develop a sense of identity and build resilience.

Conclusion:

Understanding the impact of birth order on Middle Child Syndrome is essential for educators to support middle children effectively. By recognizing the challenges they face and implementing strategies to address them, we can create a positive and empowering educational experience for middle children. Through our guidance and support, we can help them overcome Middle Child Syndrome and develop into confident, successful individuals.

Common Characteristics and Behaviors Associated with Middle Child Syndrome

In this subchapter, we will explore the common characteristics and behaviors that are often associated with the Middle Child Syndrome. As educators, it is crucial for us to understand the psychological effects of this syndrome in order to better support and nurture middle children in our classrooms.

Middle Child Syndrome refers to the unique set of challenges and experiences that middle-born individuals face within their families. These challenges arise due to their birth order and the dynamics that develop within the sibling hierarchy. Middle children often feel overlooked, overshadowed, and neglected, which can have a significant impact on their psychological well-being.

One common characteristic of middle children is a strong desire for attention and validation. They may exhibit behaviors such as seeking attention from teachers and peers, engaging in disruptive behaviors, or withdrawing from social interactions. It is important for educators to recognize these behaviors as a manifestation of their need for recognition and provide them with the support and attention they seek.

Another common behavior associated with middle children is a heightened sense of independence. Due to their position in the family, they often develop self-reliance and adaptability as a means of coping with the attention imbalance. They may display characteristics such as being resourceful, self-motivated, and capable of working well in groups or independently.

Middle children also tend to be highly empathetic and sensitive to the emotions of others. This empathy often stems from their experience of feeling overlooked and neglected, as they develop a deep understanding of the emotional needs of those around them. Educators can harness this empathetic ability by providing opportunities for middle children to support and help their peers, fostering a sense of belonging and purpose.

It is important to note that not all middle children will exhibit the same characteristics or behaviors. Each individual is unique, and their experiences both within and outside the family will shape their personality and behavior. However, by understanding the common characteristics associated with middle children, educators can create a more inclusive and supportive learning environment that meets the specific needs of these students.

By recognizing and addressing the psychological effects of the Middle Child Syndrome, educators can play a vital role in helping middle-born individuals thrive academically and emotionally. In the following chapters, we will delve deeper into various aspects of the Middle Child Syndrome, providing educators with valuable insights and strategies to support the psychological well-being and success of middle children in the classroom.

The Psychological Effects of Middle Child Syndrome on Education

Education plays a crucial role in shaping the lives of individuals, and understanding the unique challenges faced by middle-born children is essential for educators. In this subchapter, we will explore the psychological effects of Middle Child Syndrome (MCS) on education and provide insights into how educators can support and empower middle children in their academic journey.

Middle Child Syndrome refers to the psychological impact experienced by middle-born children who often feel overlooked, overshadowed, or neglected within their families. These feelings can significantly influence their educational experiences, affecting their self-perception, motivation, and overall academic performance.

One of the key psychological effects of MCS on education is the development of a unique set of traits in middle children. Research has shown that middle-borns tend to be independent, adaptable, and diplomatic, which can both positively and negatively impact their educational journey. Educators need to recognize these traits and provide opportunities for middle children to express their individuality and develop their strengths.

Additionally, sibling rivalry in middle childhood can have profound psychological implications on a middle child's educational progress. The constant comparison with older and younger siblings can lead to increased pressure, feelings of inadequacy, and self-doubt. Educators must create a supportive and inclusive classroom environment that celebrates each student's achievements and fosters healthy competition.

Furthermore, middle children often struggle with identity formation due to their birth order. Understanding the role birth order plays in self-perception can help educators tailor their teaching strategies to meet the unique needs of middle-born students. Encouraging self-reflection, providing opportunities for self-expression, and promoting a sense of belonging can positively impact their educational journey.

To nurture the psychological well-being of middle children, educators must employ effective parenting strategies in the classroom. Creating a nurturing and inclusive learning environment, offering regular feedback, and acknowledging their efforts can boost their self-esteem and motivation to succeed academically.

Middle Child Syndrome can also impact peer relationships, as middle-born individuals may struggle to find their place within social dynamics. Educators can support middle children by promoting teamwork, facilitating group activities, and fostering positive peer interactions.

Lastly, investigating the factors that contribute to achievement in middle-born individuals can help educators create targeted interventions to support their academic success. Identifying their strengths, providing appropriate challenges, and offering additional support when needed can empower middle children to reach their full potential.

In conclusion, understanding the psychological effects of Middle Child Syndrome on education is vital for educators. By recognizing the unique traits, challenges, and strengths of middle-born students, educators can create a nurturing and inclusive learning environment that supports their academic and psychological growth. By addressing the specific needs of middle children, educators can empower them to overcome the challenges associated with Middle Child Syndrome and succeed in their educational journey.

Chapter 2: Birth Order and Personality: Examining the Middle Child's Unique Traits

Birth Order Theory and Its Relevance to Middle Child Personality

Introduction:

In this subchapter, we will delve into the Birth Order Theory and its implications for understanding the personality of middle children. As educators, it is crucial for us to comprehend the psychological effects that birth order can have on our students. By exploring this theory, we can gain valuable insights into the unique traits and characteristics exhibited by middle-born individuals, enabling us to better support and guide them in their educational journey.

Understanding Birth Order Theory:

Birth Order Theory suggests that the order in which children are born within a family significantly influences their personality development. Middle children, being neither the oldest nor the youngest, occupy a unique position within the family hierarchy. This subchapter aims to shed light on how this birth order impacts their psychological well-being and overall development.

Middle Child Traits:

Middle children often exhibit distinct personality traits that are shaped by their birth order. They tend to be adaptable, diplomatic, and peacemakers. Due to their position between older and younger siblings, they learn to negotiate, compromise, and mediate conflicts. However, they may also experience feelings of being overlooked or overshadowed, leading to the development of the Middle Child Syndrome.

Relevance to Educators:

Educators play a pivotal role in recognizing and addressing the specific needs of middle-born students. By understanding the impact of birth order on personality, educators can create a supportive and inclusive learning environment. Strategies can be implemented to boost their self-esteem, encourage their unique strengths, and help them navigate through sibling rivalry or feelings of being misunderstood.

Implications for Classroom Dynamics:

Middle child students may face challenges in peer relationships and communication. Educators can explore strategies to enhance their social skills, foster positive relationships, and provide opportunities for middle-born individuals to express themselves both verbally and non-verbally. By acknowledging their birth order and the potential impact on their communication style, educators can create a more empathetic and understanding classroom environment.

Conclusion:

In conclusion, the Birth Order Theory offers valuable insights into the unique traits and characteristics of middle children. Educators must recognize the relevance of birth order to better understand the psychological effects experienced by middle-born students. By incorporating this knowledge into our teaching practices, we can support their development, nurture their well-being, and help them navigate the challenges they may face.

Middle Child Personality Traits and Characteristics

In this subchapter, we will delve into the unique personality traits and characteristics often observed in middle-born individuals. As educators, understanding these psychological effects can help us create a supportive and nurturing environment for middle children in our classrooms.

The middle child syndrome refers to the feelings of neglect, insecurity, and identity crisis that some middle children experience due to their birth order. However, it is essential to recognize that not all middle children will exhibit these traits, as personality development is influenced by various factors.

One of the key traits commonly associated with middle children is their ability to adapt and be flexible. Growing up in a family dynamic where they often have to share attention and resources with older and younger siblings, middle children learn to compromise and find their place within the family structure. This adaptability translates into their educational settings, making them more open to new experiences and ideas.

Middle children also tend to possess strong interpersonal skills. Having grown up with siblings, they have had ample opportunities to develop social skills and navigate complex relationships. They often possess excellent mediation and negotiation skills, making them natural peacemakers in the classroom.

Furthermore, middle children are often characterized by a strong sense of independence and self-reliance. This stems from their need to forge their own identity within the family structure, separate from their older and younger siblings. Educators can encourage and nurture this independence by providing opportunities for middle children to take on leadership roles and make decisions for themselves.

Middle children also tend to be highly empathetic individuals. Having experienced the challenges of being in the middle, they develop a deep understanding of others' perspectives and emotions. This empathy can be harnessed in the classroom by encouraging middle children to engage in activities that promote understanding and support for their peers.

It is important for educators to be aware of these middle child personality traits and characteristics when designing their teaching strategies. By creating an inclusive and supportive learning environment that acknowledges and values the unique qualities of middle-born individuals, we can help them thrive academically, socially, and emotionally.

In the following chapters, we will explore various aspects of middle child development, including their identity formation, peer relationships, communication styles, resilience, and success factors. By gaining a comprehensive understanding of the middle child syndrome, educators can be better equipped to meet the needs of middle children and contribute to their overall well-being and success.

The Influence of Birth Order on Middle Child's Identity Formation

Introduction:

In this subchapter, we will explore how birth order influences the identity formation of middle children. Understanding this aspect of the middle child syndrome is crucial for educators as it can significantly impact the psychological well-being of these students. By recognizing and addressing the unique challenges faced by middle-born individuals, educators can create a supportive environment that nurtures their identity development.

The Middle Child Identity Formation:

Middle children often find themselves caught between their older and younger siblings, struggling to establish their own identity. Birth order plays a pivotal role in shaping their self-perception, as they may feel overlooked or overshadowed by their siblings. This can lead to feelings of insecurity, inferiority, and a desire for validation.

Effects on Self-Perception:

Middle children tend to develop a distinct set of traits influenced by their birth order. They often exhibit strong negotiation skills, adaptability, and a desire for fairness. However, their self-perception may be affected by comparisons with their older sibling's accomplishments or the attention given to the youngest child. Educators must be attuned to these dynamics and provide opportunities for middle children to express themselves and explore their unique talents and interests.

Implications for Academic Achievement:

The influence of birth order on middle child identity formation can have a significant impact on their academic success. Middle children may feel the need to excel academically to gain recognition or prove their worth. Educators can support their achievement by providing a nurturing and inclusive classroom environment that encourages their individuality and celebrates their accomplishments.

Addressing Sibling Rivalry:

Sibling rivalry is a common phenomenon among middle children, as they compete for attention and resources. Educators can help mitigate this rivalry by promoting cooperation, conflict resolution skills, and fostering healthy relationships among siblings. By teaching empathy and understanding, educators can empower middle children to navigate the complexities of sibling dynamics and build stronger familial bonds.

Conclusion:

Understanding the influence of birth order on middle child identity formation is essential for educators. By recognizing the unique challenges faced by middle-born individuals and providing a supportive learning environment, educators can help middle children develop a strong sense of self, achieve academic success, and build healthy relationships with their siblings. By nurturing the psychological well-being of middle-born individuals, educators play a vital role in breaking the cycle of the middle child syndrome and empowering these students to thrive.

How Middle Child Personality Traits Affect Learning and Development

Introduction:

In this subchapter, we will explore how the personality traits of middle children influence their learning and development. As educators, it is crucial to understand the psychological effects of the Middle Child Syndrome and how it impacts the unique traits of middle-born individuals. By gaining insight into their experiences, we can create a supportive learning environment that caters to their specific needs.

Understanding Middle Child Syndrome:

Middle Child Syndrome refers to the psychological effects experienced by middle-born individuals due to their birth order. These effects can contribute to certain personality traits that influence learning and development. Middle children often feel overlooked, experience sibling rivalry, and struggle with identity formation. It is essential for educators to recognize these challenges and provide appropriate support.

Personality Traits and Learning:

Middle children possess distinct personality traits that affect their learning style. They are often characterized as adaptable, diplomatic, and independent. These traits can be both advantageous and challenging in the classroom. Educators should foster an environment that encourages their adaptability, values their diplomatic skills, and provides opportunities for independence.

Social Dynamics and Peer Relationships:

Middle children face unique challenges in their peer relationships. They may struggle to find their place between older and younger siblings, leading to feelings of isolation or exclusion. Educators should promote inclusive and collaborative activities that allow middle children to develop positive peer relationships and build social skills.

Communication and Expression:

Middle-born individuals may exhibit specific communication patterns influenced by their birth order. They are often skilled at mediating conflicts and expressing themselves verbally and non-verbally. Educators should encourage open communication in the classroom, providing middle children with opportunities to express their thoughts and feelings.

Resilience and Coping Mechanisms:

Middle children often develop resilience as a result of navigating the challenges they face within their family dynamics. As educators, we should recognize and foster these resilience-building traits by creating a safe and supportive learning environment. This will help middle children develop coping mechanisms and navigate adversity effectively.

Conclusion:

Understanding how middle child personality traits affect learning and development is vital for educators. By recognizing the psychological effects of the Middle Child Syndrome and the unique traits of middle-born individuals, we can create an inclusive, supportive, and effective learning environment. Through fostering their adaptability, independence, communication skills, and resilience, we can empower middle children to reach their full potential.

Chapter 3: Sibling Rivalry in Middle Childhood: Psychological Implications and Resolution Strategies

Understanding Sibling Rivalry and Its Impact on Middle Children

Sibling rivalry is a common phenomenon that occurs in many families, and it can have a significant impact on middle children. In this subchapter, we will delve into the intricacies of sibling rivalry and explore its psychological effects on middle-born individuals. As educators, it is crucial to understand this aspect of the middle child syndrome to better support and guide these students in the educational setting.

Sibling rivalry typically arises due to the competition for attention, resources, and parental affection among siblings. Middle children often find themselves caught in the middle of this rivalry, as they are sandwiched between the eldest and youngest siblings. This unique position can lead to feelings of neglect, insecurity, and a sense of not belonging, which can have profound psychological implications.

Middle children may experience a range of emotions, including jealousy, resentment, and a constant need for validation. They may feel overshadowed by their older and younger siblings, leading to low self-esteem and a diminished sense of self-worth. These psychological effects can manifest in various ways, such as academic underachievement, behavioral issues, or difficulties forming healthy peer relationships.

It is essential for educators to recognize and address these challenges to support middle children effectively. By understanding the psychological effects of sibling rivalry, educators can create a nurturing and inclusive classroom environment that fosters the middle child's unique traits. This includes providing opportunities for individual attention, acknowledging their accomplishments, and encouraging their strengths.

Furthermore, educators can help middle children develop resilience and cope with adversity. By teaching them essential life skills such as problem-solving, conflict resolution, and emotional regulation, educators can empower middle-born individuals to navigate the challenges they may face both at home and in school.

In conclusion, understanding sibling rivalry and its impact on middle children is crucial for educators. By acknowledging the psychological effects of this phenomenon, educators can create a supportive environment that nurtures the unique traits of middle-born individuals. Through empathy, guidance, and the development of resilience, educators can play a significant role in helping middle children thrive academically, socially, and emotionally.

Psychological Implications of Sibling Rivalry for Middle Children

Introduction

In this subchapter, we will explore the psychological implications of sibling rivalry specifically for middle children. Sibling rivalry is a common occurrence in families with multiple children and can have a significant impact on the middle child's psychological well-being. As educators, it is crucial to understand these implications and develop strategies to support middle children in navigating their unique experiences.

The Impact of Sibling Rivalry

Middle children often find themselves caught between their older and younger siblings, resulting in feelings of neglect, exclusion, and a lack of individual identity. The constant comparison to their siblings can lead to lower self-esteem and self-worth. They may also struggle with feelings of resentment towards both their older and younger siblings, as they perceive themselves as less favored or overlooked.

Effects on Identity Formation

The birth order plays a crucial role in shaping an individual's identity, and middle children are no exception. Being sandwiched between their siblings, they may struggle to establish their own unique persona. They may feel overshadowed by their older sibling's achievements or overwhelmed by the attention given to the youngest child. This can lead to a sense of identity crisis and difficulty in understanding their own strengths and interests.

Strategies for Educators

Educators can play a vital role in supporting middle children and mitigating the negative psychological effects of sibling rivalry. Firstly, it is important to foster a classroom environment that celebrates individuality and encourages self-expression. Providing opportunities for middle children to excel in their own way can boost their self-confidence and help them discover their unique talents.

Additionally, educators can create a safe space for middle children to express their feelings and concerns. By actively listening and validating their experiences, educators can help middle children feel heard and understood. Collaborating with parents and caregivers to develop effective communication channels can also contribute to resolving conflicts and reducing sibling rivalry.

Conclusion

Understanding the psychological implications of sibling rivalry for middle children is crucial for educators. By recognizing the unique challenges faced by middle children, we can support their identity formation, emotional well-being, and overall academic success. By implementing strategies that foster individuality, encourage open communication, and promote empathy, educators can make a significant difference in the lives of middle-born individuals.

Strategies for Resolving Sibling Rivalry and Promoting Healthy Relationships

Sibling rivalry is a common occurrence in many families, and it can have a significant impact on the psychological well-being of middle children. As educators, it is crucial for us to understand the psychological effects of sibling rivalry and be equipped with effective strategies to promote healthy relationships among middle-born individuals. In this subchapter, we will explore practical approaches to resolving sibling rivalry and nurturing positive connections between middle children and their siblings.

Firstly, it is important to acknowledge and validate the feelings and experiences of middle children. Middle-born individuals often feel overlooked or neglected, which can lead to resentment and rivalry with their siblings. By providing a safe space for middle children to express their emotions, educators can help them develop a sense of self-worth and improve their overall well-being.

One effective strategy is to promote open and honest communication within the family. Encourage siblings to express their thoughts and feelings in a respectful manner, allowing them to understand and empathize with each other's perspectives. This can be achieved through regular family meetings or structured discussions, where conflicts are addressed and solutions are sought collectively.

Another approach is to encourage siblings to engage in activities that foster collaboration and teamwork. By participating in shared interests and projects, middle children and their siblings can develop a sense of camaraderie and learn to appreciate each other's strengths. This can be achieved through group projects or team-building activities that encourage cooperation and mutual support.

It is also important to establish clear and consistent boundaries within the family. Educators can work with parents to set rules and expectations that promote fairness and equality among siblings. By treating each child as an individual and recognizing their unique qualities, middle children can develop a sense of identity and self-worth, reducing the need for rivalry.

Furthermore, educators can educate parents and siblings on the importance of positive reinforcement and praise. By acknowledging and celebrating each child's achievements, including middle children, parents can create an environment that nurtures self-esteem and encourages healthy competition rather than rivalry.

In conclusion, resolving sibling rivalry and promoting healthy relationships among middle-born individuals requires a combination of open communication, collaboration, clear boundaries, and positive reinforcement. By implementing these strategies, educators can support middle children in developing strong and positive connections with their siblings, ultimately contributing to their overall psychological well-being.

The Role of Educators in Addressing Sibling Rivalry Issues

Sibling rivalry is a common phenomenon that occurs in many families, and it can have a significant impact on the psychological well-being of the middle child. As educators, it is essential for us to understand the role we play in addressing these issues and supporting middle children who may be experiencing the effects of sibling rivalry. By recognizing the unique challenges faced by middle children and implementing effective strategies, we can help them develop a positive sense of self and navigate the complexities of their birth order.

One of the key ways educators can address sibling rivalry issues is by creating a supportive and inclusive classroom environment. Middle children often struggle with feelings of being overlooked or overshadowed by their siblings, which can affect their self-esteem and motivation to succeed academically. By fostering a sense of belonging and recognizing the individual strengths and talents of middle children, we can help them develop a strong sense of identity and confidence in their abilities.

Another important role educators play is in teaching conflict resolution skills. Sibling rivalry often stems from competition for attention, resources, and parental approval. By teaching middle children effective communication and problem-solving skills, we can empower them to navigate conflicts with their siblings in a constructive and healthy manner. This can help reduce the negative psychological implications of sibling rivalry and promote positive sibling relationships.

Furthermore, educators can also provide resources and support for parents in addressing sibling rivalry issues at home. By collaborating with parents and sharing strategies for promoting positive sibling relationships, we can create a holistic approach to addressing the psychological effects of middle child syndrome. This may include providing resources such as books, articles, and workshops that focus on sibling dynamics and effective parenting strategies specific to middle children.

In conclusion, educators play a crucial role in addressing sibling rivalry issues and supporting middle children in their psychological development. By creating a supportive classroom environment, teaching conflict resolution skills, and collaborating with parents, we can help middle children navigate the challenges of sibling rivalry and develop a strong sense of self. By understanding and addressing the unique needs of middle children, we can contribute to their overall well-being and success.

Chapter 4: Middle Child Identity Formation: Exploring the Role of Birth Order on Self-Perception

The Formation of Middle Child's Identity

Introduction:

In this subchapter, we delve into the fascinating process of the formation of a middle child's identity. Understanding how birth order influences self-perception is crucial for educators, as it allows us to tailor our approach to support and nurture these unique individuals. By examining the psychological effects of the middle child syndrome, we gain valuable insights into their development and provide them with the tools they need to thrive.

Exploring the Role of Birth Order on Self-Perception:

Middle children often face a distinct set of circumstances that shape their identity. As educators, we must acknowledge the impact of birth order on their self-perception. By recognizing the challenges they may encounter, such as feeling overlooked or overshadowed by their siblings, we can create an inclusive and nurturing learning environment that celebrates their individuality.

Examining the Middle Child's Unique Traits:

Middle children possess a range of distinctive characteristics that contribute to their identity formation. From being adaptable and diplomatic to displaying strong problem-solving skills, these traits are a result of their position in the family hierarchy. By acknowledging and encouraging these attributes, educators can empower middle children to embrace their strengths and build resilience.

Psychological Implications and Resolution Strategies for Sibling Rivalry in Middle Childhood:

Sibling rivalry is a common occurrence in middle childhood and can have lasting psychological implications if not addressed. Educators play a crucial role in guiding children towards conflict resolution strategies and fostering healthy relationships between siblings. By teaching empathy, effective communication, and negotiation skills, we can help middle children navigate the challenges of sibling rivalry and develop stronger identities.

Investigating the Factors that Contribute to Achievement in Middle-Born Individuals:

Middle children often face unique obstacles in their academic journey, but they also possess qualities that contribute to their success. By examining the factors that influence achievement in middle-born individuals, educators can identify areas where additional support may be needed. By providing personalized attention and acknowledging their accomplishments, we can foster a positive self-image and promote a growth mindset.

Conclusion:

The formation of a middle child's identity is a complex process influenced by birth order and the challenges they face within the family dynamic. As educators, it is our responsibility to understand and support their unique needs. By nurturing their strengths, fostering healthy relationships, and providing a supportive learning environment, we can empower middle children to develop a strong sense of self and thrive academically, socially, and emotionally.

Factors Influencing Middle Child's Self-Perception

Introduction:

In this subchapter, we will explore the various factors that influence a middle child's self-perception. Understanding these factors is crucial for educators in order to provide appropriate support and guidance to middle-born students. By recognizing the unique challenges and strengths of middle children, educators can foster a positive learning environment that promotes their psychological well-being.

Birth Order and Sibling Dynamics:

Middle children often experience unique challenges within their family dynamics. The order in which they are born can shape their self-perception. Being sandwiched between older and younger siblings, middle-born individuals may feel neglected or overlooked. This can lead to feelings of insecurity, low self-esteem, and a need for validation. Educators must be sensitive to these dynamics and provide opportunities for middle children to express themselves and receive recognition for their achievements.

Parenting Styles and Expectations:

Middle children may face different parenting styles and expectations compared to their older and younger siblings. Parents may be less strict with middle-born children, leading to a perception of being less important or less deserving of attention. Conversely, parents may place high expectations on middle children to excel academically or socially. These expectations can contribute to feelings of pressure and self-doubt. Educators should collaborate with parents to find a balance that supports the middle child's growth and development.

Peer Relationships and Social Dynamics:

Middle children often navigate complex social dynamics both at home and in school. They may struggle with feelings of being "stuck in the middle" and find it challenging to form strong friendships. Educators can facilitate opportunities for middle children to build social connections and develop healthy relationships. Group activities, cooperative learning, and classroom discussions can help middle-born students feel valued and supported by their peers.

Identity Formation and Self-Expression:

Birth order has a profound impact on a middle child's identity formation. They may develop unique traits such as adaptability, diplomacy, and a desire for fairness. However, middle children may also struggle with self-identity and finding their place within their family and society. Educators should encourage self-expression through creative outlets, class projects, and discussions that allow middle children to explore their interests and strengths.

Conclusion:

By understanding the factors that influence a middle child's self-perception, educators can provide the necessary support and guidance to foster their psychological well-being. Recognizing the challenges and strengths of middle children, educators can create a positive and inclusive learning environment that allows them to thrive. By working collaboratively with parents and addressing the unique needs of middle-born students, educators can help them develop a strong sense of self, resilience, and empathy.

Self-Esteem and Identity Development in Middle Children

Middle children often face unique challenges when it comes to developing a strong sense of self-esteem and identity. In this subchapter, we will explore the psychological effects of the middle child syndrome on self-perception and delve into strategies that educators can employ to support these students in their journey of self-discovery.

Birth order plays a significant role in shaping an individual's personality, and middle children are no exception. The middle child syndrome can manifest itself in various ways, including feelings of being overlooked, overshadowed by older siblings, or having inadequate attention from parents and educators. These experiences can greatly impact a middle child's self-esteem and identity formation.

To better understand the psychological implications of sibling rivalry in middle childhood, educators must recognize the detrimental effects it can have on a middle child's self-worth. It is crucial to provide a safe and supportive environment where middle children can express their feelings and concerns. By implementing resolution strategies such as mediation and conflict resolution techniques, educators can help middle children navigate through sibling rivalry and develop healthier relationships with their siblings.

Furthermore, the role of birth order in shaping self-perception cannot be overlooked. Middle children often struggle with their identity formation as they are sandwiched between older and younger siblings. Educators can facilitate discussions and activities that encourage middle children to explore their unique traits and talents, thereby fostering a stronger sense of self and promoting positive self-esteem.

Parenting strategies also play a crucial role in nurturing the psychological well-being of middle children. Educators can collaborate with parents to create a supportive network that acknowledges the middle child's individuality and provides them with opportunities for growth and development. By fostering a sense of belonging and validation, educators can help middle children build resilience and navigate the challenges they face.

In addition, social dynamics and peer relationships can greatly impact a middle child's self-esteem. Educators should be mindful of the social challenges middle children may face and create inclusive environments that facilitate positive peer interactions. By encouraging empathy and fostering a sense of belonging, educators can help middle children develop strong social skills and forge meaningful connections with their peers.

In conclusion, self-esteem and identity development are critical aspects of a middle child's psychological well-being. Educators play a pivotal role in supporting middle children as they navigate the unique challenges associated with the middle child syndrome. By understanding the psychological effects, employing effective strategies, and fostering a nurturing environment, educators can empower middle children to develop a strong sense of self-esteem and identity, ultimately setting them up for success in their academic and personal lives.

Strategies for Supporting Middle Child Identity Formation in Educational Settings

Introduction:

In educational settings, it is crucial for educators to understand and support the unique identity formation of middle children. Middle children often struggle with their place in the family and society, leading to the development of the Middle Child Syndrome. To address this issue, educators can employ various strategies to promote a healthy and positive self-perception in middle children.

1. Recognize and validate their experiences:

Educators should acknowledge the existence of the Middle Child Syndrome and its impact on middle children's psychological well-being. By validating their experiences and emotions, educators can create a safe and supportive environment for middle children to express themselves.

2. Foster positive relationships with peers and teachers:

Encourage middle children to build strong relationships with their peers and teachers. Provide opportunities for group work, collaborative projects, and team-building activities. This will help middle children develop social skills, boost their self-esteem, and promote a sense of belonging.

3. Encourage self-reflection and self-expression:

Create opportunities for middle children to explore their thoughts and feelings through journaling, art, or discussions. Encourage them to express their unique perspectives, opinions, and ideas. This will help middle children develop a strong sense of self and articulate their identities.

4. Celebrate their achievements and strengths:

Recognize and celebrate the accomplishments and strengths of middle children. Provide positive feedback and reinforcement to boost their self-confidence. Highlight their unique traits, talents, and abilities to reinforce their sense of self-worth.

5. Provide leadership opportunities:

Middle children often feel overshadowed by their older and younger siblings. Offer leadership roles in classrooms, clubs, or extracurricular activities to middle children. This will empower them and allow them to showcase their skills and abilities, fostering a sense of agency and self-assurance.

6. Offer counseling and support:

Educators should be trained to identify signs of emotional distress or self-esteem issues in middle children. Provide access to counseling services or support groups where they can share their experiences and receive guidance to cope with any challenges they may face.

Conclusion:

By implementing these strategies, educators can play a vital role in supporting the identity formation of middle children in educational settings. Recognizing their unique challenges and providing a nurturing environment will help middle children develop a strong sense of self, resilience, and success in both academic and social aspects of their lives.

Chapter 5: Middle Child Parenting: Strategies for Nurturing the Psychological Well-Being of Middle Children

Understanding the Unique Parenting Challenges of Middle Children

As educators, it is crucial for us to have a comprehensive understanding of the unique challenges faced by middle children. The middle child syndrome, often referred to as the psychological effects of being a middle-born individual, can significantly impact their development and well-being. In this subchapter, we will explore the various aspects of middle child parenting and strategies to nurture their psychological well-being.

One of the key factors influencing middle children's psychological effects is birth order and personality. Middle children often exhibit unique traits such as adaptability, diplomacy, and flexibility. It is essential for educators to recognize and appreciate these qualities to create a supportive learning environment.

Sibling rivalry is another critical aspect that affects middle children. The psychological implications of sibling rivalry can be profound, leading to feelings of neglect, low self-esteem, and a sense of being overlooked. Educators can play a vital role in resolving these issues by promoting healthy competition, fostering positive sibling relationships, and encouraging open communication among siblings.

Middle child identity formation is closely linked to birth order and self-perception. Exploring the role of birth order in shaping their identity can help educators provide appropriate guidance and support. By recognizing and valuing their unique perspective, educators can contribute to their overall well-being.

Effective parenting strategies for middle children involve creating a nurturing environment that fosters their psychological well-being. This includes fostering strong peer relationships, encouraging open and effective communication, and promoting resilience in the face of adversity. By understanding the challenges they face, educators can provide the necessary tools and resources to help middle children cope with adversity and develop resilience.

Middle children often possess exceptional empathetic abilities and characteristics. Their unique position in the family dynamic enables them to understand and relate to others' emotions. Educators can encourage and harness this empathy by fostering a culture of understanding and compassion within the classroom.

In conclusion, understanding the unique parenting challenges of middle children is crucial for educators. By recognizing the psychological effects of being a middle-born individual, birth order's impact on self-perception, and the challenges they face in peer relationships, educators can play a significant role in nurturing their psychological well-being. By implementing effective parenting strategies, promoting resilience, and encouraging empathy, educators can contribute to the overall success and happiness of middle children.

Effective Parenting Strategies for Middle Children

Middle children often face unique challenges and psychological effects due to their birth order. As educators, it is essential to understand these effects and provide support to middle children in our classrooms. This subchapter aims to provide effective parenting strategies that can nurture the psychological well-being of middle children.

One crucial strategy is to validate the middle child's feelings and experiences. Middle children often feel overlooked or overshadowed by their older and younger siblings. By acknowledging their emotions and providing them with a safe space to express themselves, parents can help middle children develop a healthy sense of self-worth.

Another strategy is to foster strong sibling relationships. Sibling rivalry can be particularly intense during middle childhood, and parents must mediate conflicts and encourage cooperation. By promoting shared activities and setting aside quality time for each child, parents can strengthen the bond between middle children and their siblings, promoting a sense of belonging and reducing feelings of rivalry.

Middle children also benefit from having their own identity within the family. Parents can encourage middle children to explore their interests and passions, supporting their unique personality traits. By providing opportunities for self-expression and individuality, parents can help middle children develop a strong sense of self and boost their self-confidence.

Communication is another essential aspect of effective parenting for middle children. Parents should create an open and supportive environment where middle children feel comfortable expressing themselves. By actively listening to their concerns and ideas, parents can validate their feelings and promote healthy communication skills.

Resilience is a crucial trait for middle children to develop, given the challenges they may face. Parents can foster resilience by encouraging problem-solving skills, teaching coping mechanisms, and providing emotional support during difficult times. By helping middle children navigate adversity and teaching them to bounce back from setbacks, parents can promote their resilience and psychological well-being.

Lastly, parents should promote empathy in middle children. By encouraging acts of kindness and teaching them to consider others' perspectives, parents can help middle children develop strong empathetic abilities. This will not only benefit their relationships with peers but also contribute to their overall psychological growth.

In conclusion, effective parenting strategies for middle children involve validating their feelings, fostering sibling relationships, promoting individuality, encouraging open communication, fostering resilience, and nurturing empathy. By implementing these strategies, educators can contribute to the psychological well-being and success of middle children in their classrooms.

The Role of Educators in Collaborating with Parents to Support Middle Children

Middle children often face unique challenges and struggles due to their birth order. As educators, it is crucial for us to understand the psychological effects of the middle child syndrome and work collaboratively with parents to support these children. By fostering a strong partnership with parents, we can create a nurturing and supportive environment that promotes the psychological well-being of middle children. This subchapter explores the role of educators in collaborating with parents to support middle children, addressing the specific needs and challenges faced by this group.

Effective collaboration between educators and parents is essential in understanding and addressing the psychological effects of the middle child syndrome. By working together, we can gain valuable insights into the child's home environment, family dynamics, and any issues that may be affecting their emotional well-being. This collaboration allows us to develop tailored strategies and interventions that cater to the unique needs of middle children.

Educators can facilitate open and honest communication with parents to create a partnership that focuses on the child's overall development. By maintaining regular communication channels, such as parent-teacher conferences and newsletters, educators can keep parents informed about their child's progress and any concerns that arise. Additionally, educators can provide resources and educational materials that help parents understand the psychological effects of the middle child syndrome and equip them with strategies to support their child effectively.

Furthermore, educators can organize workshops and seminars specifically aimed at educating parents about the unique traits and challenges faced by middle children. These sessions can provide parents with valuable insights into their child's personality and help them develop strategies to nurture their child's psychological well-being effectively.

Collaboration between educators and parents is not only crucial for addressing the challenges of the middle child syndrome but also for promoting positive peer relationships and academic success. By working together, we can create a supportive environment that encourages middle children to develop resilience, empathy, and effective communication skills. This collaboration also allows us to identify any potential issues or conflicts that may arise in peer relationships and provide the necessary guidance and support to help middle children navigate these challenges.

In conclusion, the role of educators in collaborating with parents to support middle children is vital. By fostering a strong partnership, we can create a nurturing and supportive environment that addresses the unique needs and challenges faced by middle children. Through effective communication, resources, and educational workshops, educators can empower parents with the knowledge and strategies to support their child's psychological well-being, peer relationships, and academic success.

Creating a Supportive Environment for Middle Children in Schools

Introduction:

Middle children often face unique challenges in school due to their birth order, which can impact their psychological well-being and academic success. As educators, it is crucial to understand the psychological effects of the middle child syndrome and create a supportive environment that addresses their specific needs. This subchapter will explore strategies for nurturing the psychological well-being of middle children in schools.

Understanding the Psychological Effects:

Educators need to be aware of the psychological effects of the middle child syndrome on students. Middle children may feel neglected, overlooked, or overshadowed by their older and younger siblings, leading to feelings of insecurity, low self-esteem, and frustration. By recognizing these challenges, educators can provide targeted support to help middle children thrive.

Creating a Supportive Classroom Climate:

To create a supportive environment for middle children, educators should foster a classroom climate that celebrates individuality and values each student's unique contributions. This can be achieved by encouraging open communication, active listening, and empathy among students. Providing opportunities for middle children to express themselves and share their experiences can help them develop a sense of belonging and build self-confidence.

Addressing Sibling Rivalry:

Sibling rivalry is common in middle childhood and can have adverse psychological implications for middle children. Educators should be equipped with resolution strategies to address conflicts arising from sibling rivalry. This could involve teaching conflict resolution skills, promoting cooperation rather than competition, and fostering a sense of empathy and understanding among students.

Supporting Identity Formation:

Birth order plays a significant role in shaping an individual's self-perception. Educators can support middle children's identity formation by providing opportunities for self-reflection, encouraging self-expression, and recognizing their unique strengths and talents. By helping middle children develop a positive sense of self, educators can enhance their overall well-being and academic performance.

Building Resilience:

Middle children often face adversity due to their birth order, which can impact their resilience. Educators can play a vital role in supporting middle children's resilience by teaching coping strategies, fostering a growth mindset, and providing a safe space for them to express their emotions. By equipping middle children with the tools to navigate challenges, educators can help them develop resilience and thrive academically and personally.

Conclusion:

Creating a supportive environment for middle children in schools is crucial for their psychological well-being and academic success. By understanding the psychological effects of the middle child syndrome and implementing strategies to address their unique needs, educators can create a nurturing classroom climate that supports middle children in their development, fosters positive peer relationships, and promotes their overall success.

Chapter 6: Middle Child Peer Relationships: Uncovering the Social Dynamics and Challenges

Middle Child's Social Interactions and Peer Relationships

Understanding the social dynamics and challenges that middle children face in their peer relationships is crucial for educators in fostering a supportive and inclusive learning environment. In this subchapter, we will delve into the unique aspects of middle child's social interactions and provide valuable insights for educators to better understand and address the psychological effects of the Middle Child Syndrome.

One of the key factors that influence middle children's social interactions is their birth order and the role it plays in shaping their personality. Middle children often possess unique traits such as adaptability, diplomacy, and peacemaking skills due to their position between older and younger siblings. Educators should recognize and appreciate these traits, as they can contribute positively to group dynamics and facilitate effective communication among peers.

However, middle children may also experience challenges in their peer relationships, particularly in the context of sibling rivalry. As middle children strive for recognition and attention, they may feel overshadowed by their older and younger siblings, leading to feelings of neglect or insignificance. Educators can play a crucial role in addressing these psychological implications by implementing resolution strategies that encourage open communication, empathy, and appreciation for each child's individual strengths.

Furthermore, the formation of middle child's identity is significantly influenced by their birth order. Educators should be aware of the impact this has on their self-perception and provide opportunities for middle children to explore and develop their unique identities. By acknowledging and celebrating their distinct qualities and accomplishments, educators can foster a sense of belonging and self-worth among middle-born individuals.

In terms of peer relationships, middle children may face both internal and external challenges. They may struggle with finding their place within their peer group, experiencing feelings of exclusion or being caught between the interests of older and younger peers. Educators can support middle children by creating an inclusive and supportive classroom environment that encourages collaboration, empathy, and respect for diversity.

By studying the social dynamics and challenges faced by middle children, educators can gain a deeper understanding of their students' experiences and tailor their teaching approaches accordingly. By implementing strategies that nurture the psychological well-being of middle children, educators can help them develop resilience, effective communication skills, and empathetic abilities. This subchapter aims to equip educators with valuable insights and practical strategies to create an inclusive and supportive learning environment for middle-born individuals.

Challenges Faced by Middle Children in Peer Settings

Middle children often face unique challenges in their peer settings that can have a profound impact on their psychological well-being. In this subchapter, we will explore the various difficulties middle children encounter when interacting with their peers and provide educators with valuable insights to better understand and support these students.

One of the primary challenges middle children face in peer settings is the constant struggle for attention and recognition. Sandwiched between an older and younger sibling, middle children often find themselves overshadowed by their siblings' achievements or needs. This can lead to feelings of invisibility and a diminished sense of self-worth. Educators should be mindful of these dynamics and create opportunities for middle children to shine and feel valued within the classroom.

Another significant challenge for middle children in peer settings is navigating the complex world of sibling rivalry. Middle children often experience intense competition with their siblings, which can spill over into their interactions with peers. They may struggle with feelings of jealousy, resentment, or a constant need to prove themselves. Educators can help by fostering a supportive and inclusive classroom environment that encourages cooperation rather than competition.

Furthermore, middle children may struggle with forming their own unique identity. Being sandwiched between siblings can make it challenging for them to establish a sense of individuality. In peer settings, they may feel pressure to conform and blend in rather than expressing their true selves. Educators can promote self-expression and encourage middle children to embrace their unique qualities and talents.

Additionally, middle children may face difficulties in establishing and maintaining close friendships. They may feel overlooked or struggle to assert themselves within social groups. Educators can assist by facilitating social interactions, promoting teamwork, and providing opportunities for middle children to develop their social skills.

It is essential for educators to recognize these challenges and provide targeted support to help middle children navigate peer settings successfully. By acknowledging their unique needs and fostering a nurturing environment, educators can empower middle children to develop their self-confidence, build meaningful relationships, and thrive both academically and socially.

In conclusion, middle children face several challenges in peer settings that can significantly impact their psychological well-being. By understanding these challenges and implementing appropriate strategies, educators can play a vital role in supporting middle children and helping them overcome these obstacles.

Strategies for Facilitating Positive Peer Relationships for Middle Children

Middle children often face unique challenges when it comes to forming positive peer relationships. As educators, it is crucial to understand the psychological effects of the middle child syndrome and implement strategies that can help middle children develop healthy social connections. In this subchapter, we will explore effective strategies that educators can utilize to facilitate positive peer relationships for middle children.

1. Foster an inclusive and supportive classroom environment: Create a classroom atmosphere that promotes inclusivity, empathy, and kindness. Encourage students to appreciate each other's differences and celebrate the strengths of middle children. This will help middle children feel accepted and valued by their peers.

2. Encourage cooperative learning activities: Engage middle children in group projects and collaborative tasks that require them to work together with their peers. This will provide opportunities for middle children to develop teamwork skills, build friendships, and enhance their social interactions.

3. Teach conflict resolution skills: Middle children often experience sibling rivalry, which can impact their ability to resolve conflicts effectively. Educators should teach conflict resolution strategies, such as active listening, compromise, and problem-solving, to help middle children navigate peer conflicts and develop healthy relationships.

4. Promote positive communication: Middle children may struggle with expressing themselves verbally or non-verbally due to their birth order.

Encourage open communication in the classroom and provide opportunities for middle children to practice expressing their thoughts and emotions. This can include group discussions, journaling, or role-playing activities.

5. Facilitate social skills development: Offer social skills training or workshops specifically designed for middle children. These sessions can focus on building self-confidence, assertiveness, and active listening skills. Providing middle children with the tools to navigate social situations can greatly enhance their peer relationships.

6. Encourage extracurricular involvement: Encourage middle children to participate in extracurricular activities where they can meet peers with similar interests. This can include sports, clubs, arts, or community service. By engaging in activities they enjoy, middle children can develop friendships and expand their social circles.

By implementing these strategies, educators can play a vital role in facilitating positive peer relationships for middle children. Creating an inclusive and supportive environment, teaching conflict resolution skills, promoting positive communication, facilitating social skills development, and encouraging extracurricular involvement will empower middle children to form meaningful connections with their peers. Ultimately, these strategies can help middle children overcome the challenges associated with their birth order and thrive socially and emotionally.

The Role of Educators in Promoting Inclusive Peer Environments

In any classroom setting, educators play a crucial role in shaping the social dynamics and fostering inclusive peer environments. This is especially important when it comes to middle children, who often struggle with the psychological effects of their birth order. Understanding the unique challenges faced by middle children and their role in sibling rivalry is essential for educators seeking to create a supportive and inclusive classroom environment.

Firstly, educators must recognize the psychological effects of the middle child syndrome. Middle children often feel overlooked, overshadowed by their older and younger siblings. This can lead to feelings of insecurity, low self-esteem, and a sense of being misunderstood. Educators should be sensitive to these emotions and work to create a safe space where middle children feel heard and valued.

To promote inclusive peer environments, educators can encourage open communication among students. By fostering an atmosphere of respect and empathy, educators can help middle children develop strong communication skills and build positive relationships with their peers. Additionally, educators can implement group activities and collaborative projects that encourage teamwork and cooperation, allowing middle children to feel included and valued by their classmates.

Furthermore, educators should be proactive in addressing sibling rivalry and conflicts that may arise among middle children. By teaching conflict resolution strategies and encouraging open dialogue, educators can help middle children navigate their relationships with siblings and peers in a healthy and constructive manner. This can lead to improved social skills and increased resilience in the face of adversity.

Educators should also take into account the unique traits associated with middle children when designing their teaching strategies. Middle children tend to be independent, diplomatic, and adaptable. By providing opportunities for middle children to showcase their strengths and offering flexible learning environments, educators can help middle children thrive academically and socially.

In conclusion, educators play a vital role in promoting inclusive peer environments for middle children. By understanding the psychological effects of the middle child syndrome, addressing sibling rivalry, and recognizing the unique traits of middle children, educators can create a classroom environment where all students feel valued, included, and supported.

Chapter 7: Middle Child Success: Investigating the Factors that Contribute to Achievement in Middle-Born Individuals

Academic Success and Middle Child Syndrome

In the subchapter "Academic Success and Middle Child Syndrome," we delve into the intriguing connection between birth order and academic achievement in middle-born individuals. As educators, it is imperative to understand the psychological effects of the Middle Child Syndrome and how it may impact a middle child's academic journey.

Research has shown that middle children often experience unique traits that can influence their academic performance. Middle-born individuals tend to develop strong negotiation and peacemaking skills due to their position in the family dynamic, where they often navigate conflicts between older and younger siblings. These conflict resolution skills can contribute to their success in group work and collaborative learning environments.

However, the Middle Child Syndrome can also present challenges in academic settings. Middle children may feel overlooked or overshadowed by their older and younger siblings, leading to feelings of inadequacy or lower self-esteem. This can manifest in their academic performance, where they may struggle to find their voice or assert themselves.

As educators, it is crucial to recognize and address these psychological implications. By fostering a nurturing and inclusive classroom environment, middle children can develop a sense of belonging and confidence in their abilities. Encouraging open communication and providing opportunities for middle children to express themselves both verbally and non-verbally can help them overcome the challenges associated with their birth order.

Furthermore, understanding the role of birth order on self-perception is essential in supporting middle children in their identity formation. By acknowledging and appreciating their unique strengths and characteristics, educators can empower middle-born individuals to embrace their individuality and succeed academically.

This subchapter also explores the factors that contribute to academic achievement in middle-born individuals. By investigating the interplay between birth order and academic success, educators can gain valuable insights into effective teaching strategies tailored specifically for middle children. Identifying and capitalizing on their innate resilience and empathetic abilities can further enhance their academic journey.

In conclusion, "Academic Success and Middle Child Syndrome" sheds light on the complex relationship between birth order and academic achievement. By understanding the psychological effects of the Middle Child Syndrome and implementing appropriate strategies, educators can play a pivotal role in nurturing the academic success and well-being of middle-born individuals.

Factors that Contribute to Middle Children's Achievement

Achievement in middle-born individuals is influenced by various factors that educators should understand and consider in order to effectively support and motivate these students. This subchapter explores the key elements that contribute to middle children's success and provides educators with valuable insights into how to enhance their academic and personal growth.

One significant factor that contributes to middle children's achievement is their unique traits, which are shaped by their birth order and personality. Research suggests that middle children often possess characteristics such as diplomacy, adaptability, and creativity. Educators can leverage these traits by creating a classroom environment that fosters creativity, encourages collaboration, and values different perspectives. By recognizing and capitalizing on these unique traits, educators can empower middle children to thrive academically.

Another important aspect to consider is the role of sibling rivalry in middle childhood and its psychological implications. Middle children often experience feelings of neglect or being overlooked, which can affect their self-esteem and motivation. Educators can address this by promoting a positive and inclusive classroom culture that celebrates each student's achievements and encourages healthy competition. By nurturing a sense of belonging and recognition, educators can help middle children overcome the negative effects of sibling rivalry and achieve their full potential.

Furthermore, the formation of middle child identity plays a crucial role in their achievement. Middle children are constantly comparing themselves to their older and younger siblings, which can shape their self-perception and impact their academic performance. Educators can support middle children in developing a strong sense of self by providing opportunities for self-reflection, encouraging independent thinking, and celebrating their unique strengths and accomplishments. By fostering a positive self-image, educators can empower middle children to overcome any perceived disadvantages and excel academically.

Additionally, parenting strategies have a significant impact on the psychological well-being of middle children, which in turn affects their achievement. Educators can collaborate with parents to create a supportive and nurturing home environment that fosters the development of self-confidence, resilience, and a growth mindset. By providing parents with guidance and resources, educators can ensure that middle children receive the necessary support at home to thrive in their academic pursuits.

In conclusion, understanding the factors that contribute to middle children's achievement is essential for educators seeking to provide effective support and guidance. By recognizing their unique traits, addressing the psychological implications of sibling rivalry, fostering the development of a positive self-identity, and collaborating with parents, educators can create an environment that empowers middle children to achieve their full potential.

Strategies for Fostering Middle Child Success in Education

As educators, it is crucial for us to understand the unique challenges and psychological effects that middle children face. Middle children often experience the middle child syndrome, which can impact their self-esteem, confidence, and overall success in education. However, by implementing effective strategies, we can foster middle child success in the classroom and help them reach their full potential.

One strategy is to create a positive and inclusive classroom environment. Middle children may sometimes feel overlooked or overshadowed by their older and younger siblings. By actively recognizing and valuing their contributions, we can boost their self-esteem and sense of belonging. Encourage middle children to share their thoughts and ideas, and provide opportunities for leadership roles and responsibilities.

Another important strategy is to personalize instruction and learning experiences. Middle children often have unique traits and characteristics that differ from their siblings. By understanding their individual needs and learning styles, educators can tailor their teaching methods to accommodate these middle child traits. This can enhance their engagement and motivation, leading to improved academic performance.

Furthermore, promoting healthy sibling relationships can positively impact middle child success. Sibling rivalry is common in middle childhood and can have psychological implications. Educators can address this by teaching conflict resolution strategies and encouraging empathy and understanding among siblings. By fostering positive relationships at home, we can create a supportive environment that aids in the middle child's educational journey.

Additionally, it is essential to communicate regularly with parents and guardians. Middle child parenting strategies can greatly influence a middle child's psychological well-being and academic success. By providing resources and guidance to parents, educators can ensure that they are equipped with the knowledge and skills to support their middle children effectively.

Lastly, we must celebrate and recognize the achievements of middle-born individuals. Middle child success can be influenced by various factors such as resilience, empathy, and communication skills. By highlighting and acknowledging their accomplishments, we can boost their self-confidence and motivation, ultimately fostering their overall success in education.

In conclusion, understanding the psychological effects of the middle child syndrome is crucial for educators. By implementing strategies such as creating an inclusive classroom environment, personalizing instruction, promoting healthy sibling relationships, communicating with parents, and celebrating achievements, we can foster middle child success in education. Let us empower and support middle-born individuals to thrive academically and emotionally, ensuring they reach their full potential.

Recognizing and Celebrating Middle Child Achievements

As educators, it is crucial for us to understand the psychological effects of the middle child syndrome to better support our students. In this subchapter, we will explore the importance of recognizing and celebrating middle child achievements, shedding light on the unique traits and challenges they face.

Middle children often experience feelings of neglect or being overshadowed by their siblings. They may struggle with a sense of identity and self-worth, which can impact their academic performance and overall well-being. By acknowledging and celebrating their achievements, we can help boost their confidence and provide them with a sense of validation.

One effective way to recognize middle child achievements is through public acknowledgment. Whether it is a simple mention in class or a special ceremony, such recognition can go a long way in making them feel seen and appreciated. Additionally, creating opportunities for middle children to showcase their talents and skills can help them gain recognition and develop a sense of pride in their abilities.

Another important aspect of celebrating middle child achievements is to involve their siblings and peers. By encouraging their siblings to appreciate and support their accomplishments, we can foster a positive sibling dynamic and reduce feelings of rivalry. Peer recognition and support can also play a significant role in boosting their self-esteem and sense of belonging.

Furthermore, it is essential to provide middle children with a platform to express themselves creatively. This can be done through art, writing, or other forms of self-expression. By encouraging their unique talents and interests, we can help them develop a stronger sense of self and recognize their individual worth.

In conclusion, recognizing and celebrating middle child achievements is crucial for their psychological well-being and academic success. By providing public acknowledgment, involving siblings and peers, and nurturing their creativity, we can empower middle children to overcome the challenges they face and thrive. Let us strive to create an inclusive and supportive environment that celebrates the achievements of all our students, including the middle-born individuals.

Chapter 8: Middle Child Communication: Analyzing the Impact of Birth Order on Verbal and Non-Verbal Expression

The Influence of Birth Order on Middle Child's Communication Style

Introduction:

In this subchapter, we will explore the influence of birth order on the communication style of middle children. As educators, it is essential to understand the psychological effects of birth order on middle-born individuals to better support their development and well-being. By examining their unique communication traits, we can gain valuable insights into their needs, challenges, and strengths in various social contexts.

Understanding Middle Child Communication Style:

Middle-born children often exhibit distinct communication patterns as a result of their birth order. Growing up in between older and younger siblings, they develop a unique way of expressing themselves verbally and non-verbally. Middle children frequently display exceptional negotiating skills, adaptability, and a strong desire for harmony in their relationships with peers and adults.

Challenges and Opportunities:

The communication style of middle children can be influenced by various factors, including the attention-seeking behaviors of older siblings and the nurturing role they often play for younger siblings. These experiences can shape their communication patterns and impact their ability to assert themselves effectively. Educators need to be aware of these challenges and provide opportunities for middle children to develop their communication skills in a supportive and inclusive environment.

Strategies for Enhancing Communication:

To enhance the communication skills of middle children, educators can employ specific strategies. These may include creating opportunities for middle-born individuals to practice effective communication, such as group discussions, role-playing activities, and collaborative projects. Additionally, fostering a positive and respectful classroom environment that values the contributions of all students can greatly benefit middle children in developing their communication abilities.

Collaboration with Parents:

Educators can also collaborate with parents to support the communication development of middle children. By sharing insights on the influence of birth order on communication style, educators can encourage parents to engage in open and effective communication with their middle-born child. This collaboration can help create a consistent and supportive environment that nurtures the middle child's communication skills both at home and in the classroom.

Conclusion:

Understanding the influence of birth order on middle child communication style is crucial for educators. By recognizing the unique traits and challenges faced by middle-born individuals, educators can create an inclusive and supportive learning environment that fosters effective communication skills. By working together with parents, educators can ensure that middle children receive the necessary support to develop strong communication abilities that will benefit them throughout their lives.

Verbal and Non-Verbal Communication Patterns of Middle Children

Effective communication is a vital aspect of our daily lives, and understanding the unique communication patterns of middle children can greatly assist educators in creating a supportive learning environment. Middle children often experience challenges in expressing themselves due to their birth order and the psychological effects associated with the Middle Child Syndrome. This subchapter aims to shed light on the verbal and non-verbal communication patterns of middle children, providing educators with valuable insights to enhance their teaching strategies.

Middle children, positioned between older and younger siblings, frequently develop distinct communication styles. They may demonstrate a tendency to be more adaptable and flexible in their verbal interactions, as they often need to negotiate and mediate between their siblings. These communication skills can be advantageous in the classroom, as middle children often excel in group work, collaboration, and conflict resolution.

Moreover, middle children tend to be proficient in non-verbal communication. Having grown up in an environment where they needed to understand unspoken cues from both older and younger siblings, they have honed their ability to read body language, facial expressions, and tone of voice. Educators can capitalize on this strength by incorporating activities that encourage middle children to interpret non-verbal cues, fostering their empathy and emotional intelligence.

However, it is important to note that middle children may also exhibit communication challenges. As they often feel overlooked or overshadowed by their siblings, they may struggle with asserting themselves verbally. Educators can support middle children by creating a safe and inclusive classroom environment, where their opinions and contributions are valued and encouraged.

Furthermore, middle children may resort to non-verbal communication as a means of expression. They may use gestures, facial expressions, or even physical touch to convey their emotions or seek attention. Educators need to be mindful of these non-verbal cues and provide middle children with opportunities to express themselves through alternative means, such as art, writing, or role-playing.

Understanding the unique verbal and non-verbal communication patterns of middle children is essential for educators. By recognizing and addressing these patterns, educators can foster a supportive and inclusive learning environment that allows middle children to thrive both academically and emotionally.

Enhancing Communication Skills in Middle Children Through Education

Effective communication skills are essential for success in both personal and professional relationships. Middle children, often overlooked due to their birth order, may face unique challenges in developing strong communication abilities. However, through education and support from educators, middle children can enhance their communication skills and overcome the hurdles associated with the middle child syndrome.

This subchapter aims to shed light on the importance of communication skills for middle children and provide educators with practical strategies to help them thrive. By understanding the psychological effects of the middle child syndrome, educators can tailor their teaching methods to address the specific needs of these students.

One key aspect to consider is the impact of birth order on verbal and non-verbal expression. Middle children may struggle with finding their voice and asserting themselves due to their position in the family hierarchy. Educators can create a safe and inclusive classroom environment that encourages middle children to express their thoughts and opinions freely. Additionally, incorporating activities that promote effective listening skills can help middle children become active participants in conversations and discussions.

Furthermore, educators can teach middle children essential communication techniques, such as active listening, conflict resolution, and assertiveness. These skills can empower middle children to express themselves effectively, resolve conflicts peacefully, and advocate for their needs and rights. By providing opportunities for practice and feedback, educators can help middle children refine their communication abilities and build their self-confidence.

Collaborative projects and group activities can also foster positive peer relationships and improve middle children's communication skills. Through teamwork and cooperation, middle children can learn to communicate their ideas, listen to others, and negotiate compromises. Educators can guide and mentor middle children during these activities, emphasizing the importance of effective communication and respectful interactions.

In conclusion, enhancing communication skills in middle children through education is crucial for their overall psychological well-being and success in life. Educators play a vital role in creating an inclusive and supportive learning environment that addresses the unique needs of middle children. By focusing on communication strategies and providing opportunities for practice and growth, educators can empower middle children to overcome the challenges associated with the middle child syndrome and become confident communicators.

Communicating Effectively with Middle Children in Educational Settings

Effective communication is vital in any educational setting, but when it comes to middle children, educators need to be especially mindful of their unique psychological needs. Middle children often experience the Middle Child Syndrome, which can have a profound impact on their development and academic success. In this subchapter, we will explore strategies for educators to communicate effectively with middle children, ensuring their psychological well-being and promoting positive educational outcomes.

One key aspect of effective communication with middle children is understanding their unique traits and characteristics as a result of birth order. Middle children often possess a strong desire for attention and recognition, as they often feel overshadowed by their older and younger siblings. Educators can address this by actively acknowledging and valuing the middle child's contributions, providing praise and encouragement to boost their self-esteem.

Sibling rivalry is another significant factor that can impact middle children's psychological well-being. Educators can help address this by fostering a supportive and inclusive classroom environment, where all students are encouraged to collaborate and appreciate each other's strengths. By promoting empathy and conflict resolution skills, educators can help middle children navigate the complexities of sibling dynamics and develop healthy relationships with their peers.

Middle children's identity formation is influenced by their birth order, which can impact their self-perception and self-confidence. Educators can support middle children in this process by providing opportunities for self-expression, such as group projects and presentations. By actively listening to their ideas and opinions, educators can empower middle children to develop a strong sense of self and enhance their communication skills.

Middle children often face unique challenges when it comes to their peer relationships. Educators can assist by facilitating social interactions, promoting inclusivity, and teaching social skills, such as active listening and conflict resolution. By creating a positive and supportive social environment, educators can help middle children develop meaningful connections and foster their social-emotional development.

Lastly, educators should be mindful of the potential impact of birth order on middle children's communication styles. Middle children may exhibit both verbal and non-verbal expressions that are influenced by their position in the family. By being attentive to these nuances, educators can better understand and respond to middle children's communication needs, fostering effective and meaningful dialogue.

By implementing these strategies, educators can create a supportive and empowering educational environment that addresses the unique psychological needs of middle children. Effective communication with middle children is crucial for their psychological well-being, academic success, and overall development.

Chapter 9: Middle Child Resilience: Studying How Middle Children Cope with Adversity and Develop Resilience

Adversity and Resilience in Middle Children

Middle children often face unique challenges and experiences that can significantly impact their psychological well-being. This subchapter, titled "Adversity and Resilience in Middle Children," aims to shed light on the adversities middle-born individuals may encounter and their remarkable ability to develop resilience in the face of these challenges.

Middle children, caught between the attention-seeking oldest child and the doted-upon youngest child, can sometimes feel overlooked or neglected. This feeling of being "stuck in the middle" can lead to a range of emotional challenges, including feelings of low self-esteem, identity confusion, and a sense of isolation. Educators must be aware of these potential psychological effects to effectively support middle children in their academic and personal development.

One crucial aspect to consider is the impact of sibling rivalry in middle childhood. Middle children often find themselves in the midst of intense competition and conflict with their siblings, which can leave lasting psychological implications. By understanding the underlying dynamics of sibling rivalry, educators can implement resolution strategies that promote healthy relationships and emotional well-being among middle-born students.

Moreover, birth order plays a significant role in middle child identity formation. Middle children may develop a strong sense of self based on their birth order, which can influence their behavior, interpersonal relationships, and overall outlook on life. By exploring the link between birth order and self-perception, educators can gain valuable insights into the unique traits and characteristics of middle-born students.

Middle children also face challenges in their peer relationships. The social dynamics experienced by middle children can be complex and demanding, leading to feelings of exclusion or difficulty in forming lasting connections. Educators must uncover these challenges to better support middle children in developing healthy and fulfilling relationships with their peers.

Despite these challenges, middle children have demonstrated remarkable resilience in coping with adversity. Studying how middle children develop resilience can provide educators with valuable strategies for fostering resilience in all students. By equipping middle-born individuals with the necessary tools and support, educators can help them navigate adversity and thrive both academically and personally.

In conclusion, understanding the adversities faced by middle children and their remarkable ability to develop resilience is crucial for educators. By acknowledging and addressing the unique psychological effects of the middle child syndrome, educators can create a supportive and nurturing environment that promotes the well-being and success of middle-born individuals.

Factors Influencing Middle Children's Resilience

Resilience is a crucial attribute that allows individuals to adapt, cope, and bounce back from challenging circumstances. For middle children, who often face unique psychological effects due to their birth order, developing resilience is particularly important. Educators play a vital role in understanding and supporting middle children's psychological well-being, and recognizing the factors that influence their resilience is essential in providing effective guidance. This subchapter explores the various factors that contribute to middle children's resilience and offers insights for educators to help nurture this trait.

One of the significant factors influencing middle children's resilience is their unique position within the family dynamic. Middle children often experience feelings of neglect, as they are neither the oldest nor the youngest. This sense of being overlooked can foster resilience by encouraging them to seek independence and develop self-reliance. Educators can support middle children by providing opportunities for them to take on leadership roles and encouraging their individual strengths and talents.

Sibling rivalry, another factor that impacts middle children's resilience, can both challenge and strengthen their ability to cope with adversity. Middle children often face competition for attention and resources from their older and younger siblings. This rivalry can foster resilience by teaching them conflict resolution skills, negotiation, and the importance of compromise. Educators can help middle children navigate sibling rivalry by promoting a cooperative and inclusive classroom environment that emphasizes teamwork and empathy.

The relationship between middle children and their peers also plays a crucial role in their resilience. Middle children may feel caught between their older and younger siblings, which can lead to feelings of isolation or difficulty in forming meaningful relationships with their peers. Educators can foster resilience by creating a supportive and inclusive classroom environment where middle children can connect with their peers and build social skills.

Additionally, middle children's resilience can be influenced by the level of support they receive from their parents. Educators can collaborate with parents to ensure that middle children feel valued, heard, and supported at home, which can contribute to their overall resilience. Providing resources and strategies for parents to understand and address the unique psychological effects of the middle child syndrome can be beneficial in nurturing the resilience of middle children.

Understanding the factors that influence middle children's resilience is essential for educators in supporting their psychological well-being. By recognizing their unique position within the family dynamic, addressing sibling rivalry, fostering positive peer relationships, and collaborating with parents, educators can play a vital role in helping middle children develop resilience and thrive academically and emotionally.

Resilience-Building Strategies for Middle Children in Education

Introduction:

Middle children often face unique challenges and experiences within their families and educational environments. As educators, it is crucial to understand the psychological effects of the middle child syndrome and equip ourselves with strategies to support their resilience-building journey. This subchapter aims to provide educators with practical approaches to help middle children develop resilience and thrive in their educational settings.

1. Fostering a Supportive Environment:

Create a positive and inclusive classroom environment where middle children feel valued, heard, and supported. Encourage open communication, active listening, and respect for their ideas and opinions. Foster a sense of belonging and build strong relationships between the middle child and their peers.

2. Recognizing Individual Strengths:

Middle children often strive for recognition and validation due to their unique position in the family dynamic. Acknowledge and celebrate their individual strengths and accomplishments to boost their self-esteem.

Provide opportunities for them to showcase their talents and skills, such as through class presentations, leadership roles, or participation in extracurricular activities.

3. Encouraging Self-Advocacy:

Help middle children develop their self-advocacy skills by teaching them how to express their needs, concerns, and aspirations. Provide guidance on effective communication strategies and problem-solving techniques. Encourage them to seek help when needed and empower them to take ownership of their learning journey.

4. Cultivating Resilient Mindset:

Teach middle children about the power of resilience and the importance of viewing setbacks as opportunities for growth. Foster a growth mindset by emphasizing effort, perseverance, and the ability to learn from failures. Provide them with tools and strategies to overcome challenges, such as goal-setting, time management, and stress management techniques.

5. Building Social Support Networks:

Middle children often navigate complex sibling relationships and may experience feelings of rivalry or neglect. Encourage strong peer connections and help them develop healthy friendships within the classroom. Promote teamwork, collaboration, and empathy to foster a sense of belonging and social support.

Conclusion:

By implementing these resilience-building strategies, educators can empower middle children to overcome the challenges associated with their birth order and develop the necessary skills to thrive academically, socially, and emotionally. By understanding the unique psychological effects and providing targeted support, educators play a crucial role in nurturing the psychological well-being of middle children and helping them reach their full potential.

Supporting Middle Children in Developing Resilience

Middle children often face unique challenges as they navigate their place within the family dynamic. Understanding and addressing the psychological effects of the middle child syndrome can greatly contribute to their overall well-being and success. In this subchapter, we will explore strategies and techniques that educators can employ to support middle children in developing resilience.

Resilience is the ability to bounce back from adversity and cope with life's challenges. Middle children, due to their birth order and position within the family, may experience feelings of neglect, being overlooked, or being caught in the middle of sibling rivalries. These experiences can impact their self-esteem, confidence, and overall emotional well-being. However, with the right guidance and support, middle children can develop resilience and thrive.

One effective approach is to foster a sense of belonging and significance within the classroom environment. Educators can create opportunities for middle children to feel valued and recognized for their unique strengths and contributions. This can be achieved by assigning leadership roles, encouraging peer collaboration, and providing individualized attention and feedback.

Empathy plays a crucial role in the development of resilience. Middle children may have a heightened sense of empathy due to their experiences of being caught between older and younger siblings. Educators can nurture this empathy by incorporating lessons and activities that promote understanding and compassion. By encouraging middle children to empathize with others, they can develop a greater sense of self-awareness and emotional intelligence.

It is also important to teach middle children coping mechanisms and stress management techniques. Educators can provide tools such as mindfulness exercises, problem-solving strategies, and positive self-talk to help middle children regulate their emotions and navigate challenging situations. By equipping them with these skills, educators empower middle children to face adversity with resilience and confidence.

Furthermore, building strong relationships with middle children and fostering open communication can create a safe space for them to express their thoughts and feelings. Educators can provide a listening ear, validate their experiences, and offer guidance and support when needed. By establishing a trusting relationship, educators can help middle children develop a sense of belonging and self-worth.

In conclusion, supporting middle children in developing resilience is crucial for their psychological well-being and overall success. By implementing strategies that foster a sense of belonging, empathy, coping skills, and open communication, educators can empower middle children to navigate the challenges they face and develop resilience that will serve them throughout their lives.

Chapter 10: Middle Child Empathy: Examining the Empathetic Abilities and Characteristics of Middle-Born Individuals

The Role of Birth Order in Middle Child Empathy

Empathy is an essential social skill that plays a significant role in our interactions with others. As educators, it is crucial to understand how birth order influences the development of empathy in middle-born children. In this subchapter, we will delve into the unique characteristics and empathetic abilities of middle children, shedding light on their psychological well-being.

Research suggests that middle children often possess exceptional empathetic abilities. Growing up sandwiched between older and younger siblings, they are constantly exposed to different perspectives, emotions, and needs. This exposure fosters a heightened awareness of others' feelings and a deep understanding of the complexities of human emotions.

Middle children often act as mediators in sibling disputes, honing their ability to see multiple sides of an argument. This experience allows them to develop strong conflict resolution skills and empathy for others' points of view. As educators, we can harness these skills by encouraging middle children to take on leadership roles in group activities, promoting their natural inclination towards empathy and understanding.

Furthermore, middle children's empathetic nature may stem from their experiences of feeling overlooked or overshadowed by older or younger siblings. This sense of being in the middle can cultivate a deep sense of empathy for others who may also feel overlooked or unheard. As educators, we can validate their experiences and create a safe space where middle children can express their emotions freely, fostering their empathy towards others.

It is important to note that birth order is just one factor that influences a child's empathetic development. Other factors, such as parental modeling and the overall family dynamics, also play a significant role. However, understanding the impact of birth order can provide educators with valuable insights into the empathetic abilities of middle-born individuals.

In conclusion, middle children often exhibit remarkable empathetic abilities due to their unique position in the family hierarchy. Their experiences of mediating conflicts and feeling overshadowed by siblings contribute to their heightened understanding of others' emotions. As educators, we can nurture and harness their empathetic nature by providing opportunities for leadership and creating a supportive environment that values their experiences. By understanding the role of birth order in middle child empathy, we can better support the psychological well-being and social development of middle-born individuals.

Empathy Development in Middle Children

Understanding the psychological effects of the middle child syndrome is essential for educators who work with students in this birth order position. Middle children often experience unique challenges and have distinct characteristics that can impact their emotional development, including their ability to empathize with others. In this subchapter, we will explore the development of empathy in middle children and its importance in their overall psychological well-being.

Middle children, caught between the attention-seeking older siblings and the attention-demanding younger ones, often feel overlooked or ignored. This dynamic can lead to feelings of isolation and a desire to find connection and understanding from others. Consequently, middle children may develop a heightened sense of empathy as a way to bridge this emotional gap.

Research suggests that middle children tend to be more attuned to the emotions of others and are skilled in deciphering non-verbal cues. They often possess a developed ability to understand and share the feelings of their peers, making them natural mediators and peacekeepers in social situations. Educators can harness these empathetic abilities by encouraging middle children to engage in activities that promote empathy, such as group discussions, cooperative projects, and role-playing exercises.

To further enhance empathy development in middle children, educators can create a classroom environment that fosters emotional intelligence. This can be achieved through regular discussions about emotions and feelings, encouraging students to express their thoughts and concerns, and modeling empathetic behavior. By providing opportunities for middle children to practice empathy through understanding and supporting their peers, educators can help them develop stronger emotional connections and build lasting relationships.

It is important to note that while middle children may naturally possess empathetic abilities, they still require guidance and support from educators. Recognizing and acknowledging their empathetic qualities, validating their emotions, and teaching them effective communication skills can go a long way in nurturing their overall psychological well-being.

In conclusion, empathy development in middle children is a crucial aspect of their psychological growth and social interactions. By understanding the unique characteristics and challenges faced by middle children, educators can play a vital role in fostering empathy and creating a supportive environment that enables middle-born individuals to thrive emotionally.

Promoting Empathy in Middle Children through Education

Empathy is a crucial social skill that helps individuals understand and connect with others on a deeper level. For middle children who often experience feelings of neglect or being overlooked, developing empathy can be particularly beneficial. In this subchapter, we will explore how educators can play a vital role in promoting empathy among middle children and ultimately enhance their psychological well-being.

Firstly, educators can incorporate empathy-building activities into their curriculum. By designing lessons that encourage students to step into the shoes of others and see the world from different perspectives, middle children can develop a heightened sense of empathy. For instance, teachers can assign projects that require students to research and present on diverse cultures, challenges faced by marginalized communities, or personal narratives that foster empathy and understanding.

Furthermore, educators can create a nurturing and inclusive classroom environment that values empathy. This can be achieved by fostering open discussions and encouraging students to listen and respect each other's opinions. By modeling empathetic behavior themselves, teachers can set an example for middle children, teaching them how to respond to others' emotions with kindness and understanding.

In addition, educators can also provide opportunities for middle children to engage in community service or volunteer work. Participating in activities that involve helping others allows middle children to experience the joy of making a positive impact on someone's life. By actively contributing to their community, middle children can develop a sense of empathy and social responsibility.

Moreover, incorporating literature and media that highlight empathy and compassion can be an effective strategy. By reading books or watching movies that portray characters who display empathy, middle children can learn from these role models and develop their own empathetic abilities. Educators can facilitate discussions around these stories, encouraging students to reflect on the characters' actions and emotions.

By implementing these strategies, educators can empower middle children to develop empathy, ultimately fostering their psychological well-being. As middle children navigate the unique challenges associated with their birth order, cultivating empathy can help them build stronger relationships, communicate effectively, and navigate social dynamics with greater ease. By prioritizing empathy in the education of middle children, educators can contribute to their overall growth and development, helping them thrive academically, socially, and emotionally.

Cultivating Empathy and Understanding in Educational Environments

In the realm of education, it is crucial for educators to not only impart knowledge but also to foster empathy and understanding in their students. This subchapter focuses on the unique challenges and opportunities that arise when working with middle-born individuals who often experience the middle child syndrome. By understanding the psychological effects of this syndrome, educators can create a supportive and inclusive learning environment that nurtures the emotional well-being of all students.

The middle child syndrome refers to the psychological impact of being sandwiched between older and younger siblings. Middle-born individuals often struggle with feelings of neglect, invisibility, and a lack of identity. As educators, it is essential to recognize and address these issues to ensure that middle-born students receive the attention and support they need to thrive academically and emotionally.

One effective strategy for cultivating empathy and understanding in educational environments is by creating opportunities for middle-born students to share their experiences and perspectives. By encouraging open discussions about birth order and its impact on identity formation, educators can help students develop a sense of belonging and validation. Additionally, educators can incorporate literature, films, and other resources that highlight the experiences of middle-born individuals, allowing students to explore and empathize with characters who share similar challenges.

Another important aspect to consider is the role of sibling rivalry in middle childhood. Educators should be aware of the psychological implications of sibling rivalry and provide resolution strategies to help middle-born students navigate conflicts and develop healthy relationships with their siblings. By teaching conflict resolution skills and promoting empathy among students, educators can contribute to the development of strong interpersonal skills that will benefit middle-born individuals throughout their lives.

Moreover, educators should be mindful of the impact of birth order on middle child communication. Middle-born individuals may express themselves differently, both verbally and non-verbally, compared to their older or younger siblings. By recognizing these differences and adapting teaching methods and communication styles accordingly, educators can create an inclusive learning environment that values and respects the diverse forms of expression.

In conclusion, cultivating empathy and understanding in educational environments is essential for the psychological well-being and academic success of middle-born students. By acknowledging the unique traits and challenges associated with the middle child syndrome, educators can create a supportive and inclusive learning environment that celebrates the individuality of each student. Through open discussions, resolution strategies, and adapting communication styles, educators can foster empathy and understanding among all students, ultimately contributing to their personal growth and success.

Conclusion: The Role of Educators in Supporting Middle Children's Psychological Well-Being

Recap of Key Findings and Insights

In this subchapter, we will recap the key findings and insights discussed throughout the book, "The Middle Child Syndrome: A Guide for Educators on Understanding the Psychological Effects." This book aims to provide educators with a comprehensive understanding of the middle child syndrome, its psychological effects, and strategies to support middle children in their educational journey. The following sections summarize the major takeaways from each chapter:

The Middle Child Syndrome: Understanding the Psychological Effects

- Middle children often experience feelings of neglect, lack of attention, and identity struggles.

- They may exhibit traits such as independence, diplomacy, and adaptability due to their unique position in the family.

Birth Order and Personality: Examining the Middle Child's Unique Traits

- Middle-born individuals tend to develop strong negotiation and compromise skills.

- They often possess a desire for fairness and justice due to their experiences with sibling rivalry.

Sibling Rivalry in Middle Childhood: Psychological Implications and Resolution Strategies

- Sibling rivalry can have negative psychological effects on middle children, leading to feelings of resentment and low self-esteem.

- Educators can implement conflict resolution strategies to help middle children navigate sibling rivalries and build positive relationships.

Middle Child Identity Formation: Exploring the Role of Birth Order on Self-Perception

- Middle children may struggle with developing a sense of identity due to their position between older and younger siblings.

- Educators can support middle children by fostering self-reflection, encouraging self-expression, and providing opportunities for individual growth.

Middle Child Parenting: Strategies for Nurturing the Psychological Well-Being of Middle Children

- Educators play a vital role in supporting middle children by collaborating with parents and creating a positive and inclusive classroom environment.

- Strategies such as active listening, individualized attention, and recognizing middle child strengths can contribute to their psychological well-being.

Middle Child Peer Relationships: Uncovering the Social Dynamics and Challenges

- Middle children face unique challenges in peer relationships, including feeling overlooked or struggling to find their place within social groups.

- Educators can facilitate inclusive and supportive peer interactions by promoting empathy, encouraging teamwork, and providing opportunities for social engagement.

Middle Child Success: Investigating the Factors That Contribute to Achievement in Middle-Born Individuals

- Middle-born individuals have the potential for great success, often attributed to their resilience, adaptability, and negotiation skills.

- Educators should recognize and nurture middle children's strengths while providing opportunities for personal and academic growth.

Middle Child Communication: Analyzing the Impact of Birth Order on Verbal and Non-Verbal Expression

- Birth order can influence middle children's communication styles, including a tendency to be diplomatic and assertive.

- Educators can support middle children in developing effective communication skills through practice, feedback, and modeling.

Middle Child Resilience: Studying How Middle Children Cope with Adversity and Develop Resilience

- Middle children often develop resilience through navigating their unique position in the family and overcoming challenges.

- Educators can foster resilience by creating a supportive and encouraging learning environment that celebrates effort and growth.

Middle Child Empathy: Examining the Empathetic Abilities and Characteristics of Middle-Born Individuals

- Middle-born individuals tend to possess heightened empathy due to their experiences with sibling dynamics and mediation.

- Educators can promote empathy in middle children by providing opportunities for perspective-taking, cooperative learning, and community service.

In conclusion, this subchapter provides a recap of the key findings and insights discussed throughout the book, offering educators a comprehensive understanding of the middle child syndrome and strategies to support middle children's psychological well-being and academic success. By implementing the knowledge gained from this book, educators can play a crucial role in ensuring the holistic development of middle-born individuals.

Recommendations for Educators

As educators, it is crucial for us to understand the psychological effects of the Middle Child Syndrome and its impact on our students. By familiarizing ourselves with the unique traits and challenges faced by middle-born individuals, we can create an inclusive and supportive learning environment that nurtures their psychological well-being. Here are some recommendations for educators to consider:

1. Foster a sense of belonging: Middle children often struggle with their identity due to their birth order. Encourage classroom activities that celebrate individuality and promote a sense of belonging. Create opportunities for middle-born students to share their experiences and perspectives, allowing them to feel valued and heard.

2. Address sibling rivalry: Sibling conflicts can have a significant impact on middle children's psychological well-being. Educators should intervene and mediate conflicts, teaching conflict resolution skills and promoting empathy and understanding among siblings. Provide resources and workshops for parents to help them address sibling rivalry effectively.

3. Promote positive peer relationships: Middle children may face challenges in forming and maintaining friendships. Encourage cooperative learning activities and group projects that foster collaboration and teamwork. Teach social skills and conflict resolution strategies to help middle-born students navigate peer relationships successfully.

4. Encourage resilience and coping skills: Middle children often develop resilience as a result of their unique position in the family dynamic. Help them build on this innate resilience by teaching stress management techniques, problem-solving skills, and positive coping strategies. Foster a growth mindset and encourage them to see challenges as opportunities for growth.

5. Individualize instruction: Recognize that each student is unique, and their birth order may influence their learning preferences and communication styles. Adapt your teaching strategies to accommodate different learning styles and provide opportunities for both verbal and non-verbal expression. Offer a variety of activities and assessments to cater to the diverse needs of middle-born students.

6. Cultivate empathy: Middle-born individuals often possess strong empathetic abilities. Incorporate empathy-building activities into the curriculum to help students develop their empathetic skills further. Encourage them to consider different perspectives and engage in acts of kindness and compassion.

By implementing these recommendations, educators can make a significant difference in the lives of middle-born students. Understanding the psychological effects of the Middle Child Syndrome and tailoring our teaching methods accordingly will help middle children thrive academically, socially, and emotionally. Together, let's create a supportive and empowering environment that celebrates the unique traits and strengths of middle-born individuals.

Future Research Directions

As educators, it is crucial for us to stay updated on the latest research findings and trends in order to better understand and support our students. The field of psychology has made significant progress in studying the effects of the Middle Child Syndrome, birth order, and sibling dynamics. However, there are still many avenues for future research that can deepen our understanding of these topics and help us provide more effective interventions and support strategies for middle-born children. This subchapter explores some potential future research directions that can contribute to the existing body of knowledge.

One area that warrants further investigation is the impact of birth order on the self-perception and identity formation of middle children. While previous research has touched on this topic, there is a need for more in-depth studies that explore how birth order influences middle child's sense of self, their values, aspirations, and how they navigate their social and academic environments. Understanding these dynamics can help educators tailor their teaching strategies to meet the unique needs of middle-born students.

Another important area for future research is the role of parenting in nurturing the psychological well-being of middle children. Parenting styles and strategies can have a significant impact on a child's development, and middle children may require specific approaches that differ from their older and younger siblings. Exploring effective parenting strategies, understanding the challenges faced by middle child parents, and providing resources and support can greatly enhance the overall well-being of middle-born children.

Additionally, research on middle child peer relationships can shed light on the social dynamics and challenges faced by middle children. This can include studying the impact of birth order on friendship formation, peer acceptance, and the development of social skills. Understanding these dynamics can help educators create inclusive classroom environments that foster positive peer interactions and support the social development of middle-born students.

Furthermore, investigating the factors that contribute to the success and achievement of middle-born individuals can provide valuable insights for educators. This can include exploring their motivation, resilience, and coping mechanisms in the face of adversity. Understanding these factors can help educators provide targeted support and interventions to enhance the academic and personal success of middle-born students.

Research on middle child communication, empathy, and resilience is also essential. Analyzing the impact of birth order on verbal and non-verbal expression, empathetic abilities, and characteristics of middle-born individuals can provide valuable insights into their unique communication styles and emotional intelligence. This knowledge can help educators create more effective communication strategies and foster empathy among middle-born students.

In conclusion, the field of psychology has made significant strides in understanding the Middle Child Syndrome and its psychological effects. However, there are still many areas that require further research to better support middle-born children. Future research should explore topics such as middle child identity formation, parenting strategies, peer relationships, success factors, communication styles, resilience, and empathy. By delving deeper into these areas, educators can gain a more comprehensive understanding of the unique needs and strengths of middle-born students, allowing us to provide the best possible support and guidance.